Contents

GLOBAL EVENTS

BRITISH EVENTS

Massacre at Sharpeville

At about 1.40 in the afternoon, South African police fired machine guns, rifles and revolvers into a crowd of several thousand men, women and children. The crowd fled, but the police continued to fire. Of the 69 dead and 300 injured, many were shot in the back.

The massacre ended a stand-off which had begun early that morning when black demonstrators surrounded the police station at Sharpeville. The station was protected by a wire fence, 200 heavily armed policemen and Saracen armoured cars. During the morning, more and more people arrived. The police were reinforced and a few arrests were made without any resistance being offered. The only independent witnesses described the crowd as good-humoured and not expecting trouble, although some children flung a few stones. It seems certain that nobody was armed. Unnerved by the size and movements of the crowd, the police opened fire, apparently without receiving orders to do so.

Apartheid

The Sharpeville massacre had a great impact on world opinion. It confirmed the brutally racist nature of South Africa, a country run by and for the white minority. The black majority had no vote and were mostly very poor. In theory, South Africa was not racist, but followed a policy of

Sharpeville: security forces move in after the massacre. For a long time the South African authorities tried to blame the victims, rather than their own forces, for what had happened.

Dates of a Decade

THE 1960s

Nathaniel Harris

W
FRANKLIN WATTS
LONDON • SYDNEY

First printed in paperback in 2013

First published in 2008 by Franklin Watts

Franklin Watts
338 Euston Road
London NW1 3BH

Franklin Watts Australia
Level 17/207 Kent Street, Sydney, NSW 2000

Produced by Arcturus Publishing Limited,
26/27 Bickels Yard, 151–153 Bermondsey Street,
London SE1 3HA

Series concept: Alex Woolf
Editor and picture researcher: Alex Woolf
Designer: Phipps Design

Picture credits:
Corbis: 5 (Hulton-Deutsch Collection), 7 (Bettmann), 8 (Bettmann), 9, 10 (© The
Andy Warhol Foundation for the Visual Arts, Inc. / DACS, London, 2007. Trademarks
Licensed by Campbell Soup Company. All Rights Reserved.), 11 (© Bridget Riley,
all rights reserved / Hulton-Deutsch Collection), 12, 13 (Bettmann), 14 (Bettmann),
15 (Flip Schulke), cover (right) and 16 (Bettmann), 18 (Bettmann), 19 (Bettmann),
20 (Bettmann), 21 (Tim Page), 24 (Bettmann), 25 (Bettmann), 27 (Hulton-Deutsch
Collection), 28 (Bettmann), 30 (Hulton-Deutsch Collection), 31 (Burlot
Jacques/Sygma), 32 (Alain Nogues/Sygma), cover (bottom) and 33 (epa), cover
(top) and 35, 36 (Christine Spengler/Sygma), 37 (Michael Brennan), 39 (Henry
Diltz), 45 (Bettmann).
Getty Images: 23 (Hulton Archive), 26 (Hulton Archive), 38 (Time & Life Pictures),
40 (Hulton Archive), 41 (Hulton Archive), 42 (Hulton Archive), 43 (Hulton Archive),
44 (Hulton Archive).
Rex Features: 17 (Everett Collection).
Science Photo Library: 34 (NASA).
Topham Picturepoint: 4.

Every attempt has been made to clear copyright. Should there be any inadvertent
omission, please apply to the publisher for rectification.

A CIP catalogue record for this book is available from the British Library.

Dewey Decimal Classification Number: 909.82' 6

ISBN 978 1 4451 1880 2

Printed in China

Franklin Watts is a division of Hachette Children's Books,
an Hachette Livre UK company.
www.hachettelivre.co.uk

Supplier 03, Date 0213, Print Run 2353
SL000836EN

apartheid: the different races would live and develop in separate communities, including 'homelands' set aside for black Africans. But these homelands were all poor, overcrowded areas where it was hard to make a living. In practice, 'all-white' towns and industries needed black labour, so black workers were assembled in 'townships' like Sharpeville just outside them. Townships were large but primitively equipped settlements rather than true towns.

Black Africans who lived and worked outside the homelands had to carry a passbook – a kind of identity card – at all times. Passbooks restricted their movements and separated families. They became one of the most bitterly resented symbols of oppression, and the demonstration at Sharpeville was part of a nationwide protest against the pass laws.

For whites only: as the sign makes clear, this Cape Town beach is for public use, but only by whites. Such unfair discrimination was typical of South Africa's system of apartheid (separation).

After Sharpeville

After the shooting, the South African government remained unyielding. All black political movements were outlawed and no concessions were made. Apartheid seemed immovable until the late 1980s, when it began to crumble. Finally, in 1990, the imprisoned black leader Nelson Mandela was released and South Africans set out on the road to democracy.

⊙ eye witness

The crowd seemed perfectly amiable…. Then the shooting started. We heard the chatter of a machine gun, then another, then another…. One woman was hit about ten yards from our car. Her companion, a young man, went back when she fell. He thought she had stumbled. Then he turned her over and saw that her chest had been shot away. He looked at the blood on his hand and said: 'My God, she's gone!' Hundreds of kids were running, too.

Humphrey Tyler, assistant editor of the South African magazine *Drum*, writing in the 21 March 1960 issue

- **SEE ALSO**
  Pages 6–7: 30 June 1960:
  The Congo Gains its Independence
  Pages 14–15: 28 August 1963:
  The 'I Have a Dream' Speech

- **FURTHER INFORMATION**
- 📖 Books:
  Sharpeville by Sarah Harris
  (Dryad, 1998)
- 🖱 Websites:
  http://www.sahistory.org.za/topic/sharpeville-massacre-21-march-1960
  The Sharpeville massacre, with eye-witness accounts

30
JUNE
1960

The Congo Gains its Independence

For 80 years, the Congo, a vast area in central Africa, was a colony ruled by Belgium. The colonial rulers benefited greatly from the colony's mineral wealth, yet did little to educate or improve the lives of the overwhelming majority of black Congolese. Growing discontent alarmed the Belgians, who decided that it was time to leave. Hasty elections were held, and on 30 June 1960, Patrice Lumumba, the leader of the largest political party, became prime minister of the new state. The independence ceremony revealed how differently Belgians and black Africans viewed the colonial past (see panel).

⊙ eye witness

It might have been guessed that the launching of the new Republic of Congo would prove a stormy affair…. The King declared, 'For eighty years Belgium has sent your land the best of her sons…. It is your job, gentlemen, to show that we were right in trusting you'. Lumumba … spoke many times of the 'indispensable struggle to put an end to the humiliating slavery which was imposed on us by force…. Who will forget the rifle-fire from which so many of our brothers perished, or the gaols in to which they were brutally thrown?'

The special correspondent of *The Guardian*, 1 July 1960

Chaos and conflict

Such a rapid and unprepared handover was bound to cause trouble. Almost at once, fighting broke out between different Congolese groups. Europeans were attacked, and the army mutinied against its white officers. On 11 July, the president of the copper-rich Katanga province, Moise Tshombe, announced that the province had broken away from the Congo. A very confused situation developed in which Congolese politicians vied for power while their forces tried to recover Katanga. Belgian and United Nations troops became involved, and great power rivalries even came into play when Lumumba secured help from the Soviet Union. However, Lumumba lost the struggle. He was imprisoned and then handed over to Katanga, where he was killed, supposedly trying to escape.

Fighting went on until 1963, when Katanga admitted defeat. The unity of the Congo had been preserved, but General Sese Seko Mobutu, head of the Congolese army, emerged as the real power in the country. In 1965, Mobutu thrust the politicians aside, made himself president of Zaire (as the Congo was now called), and began a 32-year reign of tyranny and corruption.

The doomed premier: Congo's first elected prime minister, Patrice Lumumba, under arrest, his arms tied behind him. Having lost a power struggle with the president, Lumumba was held by the troops of army chief Mobutu, beaten in front of television cameras, and handed over to his enemies in Katanga, where he was executed in January 1961.

Decolonization

The Congo was a chaotic example of decolonization – the end of rule by European states over most of Africa. Decolonization began in 1957, when Britain's Gold Coast colony became independent as Ghana, and continued all through the 1960s. By 1974 the colonial era was over. But in two former colonies, South Africa and Rhodesia (now Zimbabwe), the white minorities living in the country clung on to power for much longer. Africa remained a troubled continent. Most of the newly independent states either opted for single-party rule or experienced frequent military coups. In the 1970s many of them slid into debt, with serious consequences, including poverty and instability, that were still enduring economic problems in the early 21st century.

- **SEE ALSO**
  Pages 4–5: 21 March 1960: Massacre at Sharpeville
  Pages 24–25: 30 May 1967: Biafra Breaks Away from Nigeria

- **FURTHER INFORMATION**
  Books:
  Democratic Republic of the Congo by Joseph Ransford Oppong and Tania Woodruff (Chelsea House Publishers, 2007)
  Websites:
  http://historyworld.net/wrldhis/plaintext histories.asp?historyid=ad34
  History of the Democratic Republic of Congo

The Berlin Wall Rises

East German forces set to work early in the morning, long before it was light. By the time most citizens of Berlin were up, the East Germans had surrounded the western part of the city with barbed wire. Within a week the barbed wire had largely been replaced by a wall of concrete. Eventually this Berlin Wall would become a still more formidable barrier, with watch towers manned by armed guards who shot at anyone who tried to cross into West Berlin without authorization. Over the next 28 years, hundreds would be killed attempting to escape from the East to the West.

The Cold War

Berlin was on the front line in the Cold War being waged between the Western, US-led alliance and the Eastern, Soviet-led bloc. It was 'cold' because mutual hostility never turned into a 'hot', shooting war between major powers – although their growing nuclear arsenals caused worldwide alarm. In Europe, the most sensitive Cold War frontier ran between the pro-Western German Federal Republic (West Germany) and the German Democratic Republic (East Germany), which belonged in the Soviet camp.

Berlin's situation was exceptional. As a result of arrangements made between the victorious powers after World War II (1939–1945), West Berlin was part of the Federal Republic, though it lay deep inside East Germany.

Building the Berlin Wall: a construction worker adds more large blocks to the steadily rising wall, designed to prevent discontented East German citizens from fleeing to West Berlin, part of the rival West German state.

What the papers said

The scream of sirens and the clank of steel on cobblestones echoed down the mean, dark streets. Frightened East Berliners peeked from behind their curtains to see military convoys stretching for blocks…. When dawn came … a wall divided East Berlin from West Berlin…. The Wall was illegal, immoral and strangely revealing – illegal because it violated the Communists' solemn contracts to permit free movement throughout the city; immoral because it virtually jailed millions of innocent people; revealing because it advertised to all the world the failure of East Germany's Communist system.

Time, 25 August 1961

John F Kennedy, US president, views the wall from West Berlin, 26 June 1963. He is about to deliver a famous speech in praise of the hard-pressed Berliners.

It became an outpost of the Western way of life, which was visibly freer and more prosperous than the communist system imposed by the Soviet Union on East Germany and other East European states. In spite of severe travel restrictions, East Germans fled to the West in huge numbers (2.5 million between 1949 and 1961), embarrassing the government and undermining the economy.

The easiest way to leave East Germany was by slipping through the city's streets, gardens and canals into West Berlin. In July 1961, a time of East-West political tension, a staggering 30,000 East Germans left. The rapid erection of the Berlin Wall was the response – supposedly to keep out spies and saboteurs, but actually to keep the citizens in. The Western powers protested, and US President John F Kennedy made a famous speech declaring his solidarity with the beleaguered Berliners. But there was nothing to be done without risking war. The Berlin Wall stood until the 1989–1990 collapse of the communist system it was built to protect.

SEE ALSO
Pages 12–13: 22 October 1962: The Cuban Missile Crisis
Pages 32–33: 20 August 1968: Soviet Forces Invade Czechoslovakia

FURTHER INFORMATION
Books:
The Berlin Wall by Anne Rooney (Franklin Watts, 2011)
Websites:
http://userpage.chemie.fu-berlin.de/BIW/wall.html
The Berlin Wall, with links to photos

Soup Cans Sighted in Los Angeles

On 9 July 1962, the Ferns Gallery in Los Angeles, USA, staged the first one-man show by Andy Warhol, an artist who was still little known. Each of the 32 paintings in the exhibition was a careful copy of a Campbell's soup can; the only difference between one picture and the next was the variety of soup named on the painted label. The show made an impact, impressing some spectators and puzzling or annoying others. When it moved to New York in the autumn, it became an undoubted success. Within a remarkably short time, Andy Warhol became the superstar of the movement known as Pop art.

Pop art

Pop art was controversial and, some thought, not art at all. It drew heavily on well-known images from the mass media such as movies, TV, advertising and comic books. Its typical subjects were celebrities and pin-ups, cars, food and other everyday branded consumer goods. It was bright, often gaudy, and usually cheerful. These qualities, along with the familiarity of its images, gave Pop art a wider public appeal than most art movements. It was excitingly modern minded and consumption conscious, reflecting the prosperity of the 1960s and the optimism and irreverence of a period when young people had more freedom and money to spend than ever before.

A Campbell's soup can, tomato variety: one of the repeated images that made Andy Warhol a famous Pop artist.

Comic books and giant hamburgers

Some artists had been working in Pop-like styles from the mid-1950s, but 1962 was the year Pop art took off. Roy Lichtenstein's exhibition showed the works that made him, after Warhol, the most famous Pop artist – paintings of comic-book scenes, greatly enlarged but complete with the 'balloons' that told readers what a character was saying or thinking. Lichtenstein even painted in the visible dots that made up the original, crudely printed image. The Swedish-born sculptor Claes Oldenburg also came to the fore in 1962. He exhibited giant hamburgers, and also achieved unusual effects with soft vinyl versions of objects such as typewriters.

Many Pop artists not only admired mass-media images but copied the mechanical methods used to reproduce them. Warhol used a technique known as screen-printing to produce multiple images of celebrities such as the film star Marilyn Monroe, singer Elvis Presley and Chinese leader Mao Zedong. Britain also produced many Pop artists, including Richard Hamilton, Peter Blake and Allen Jones. The style dominated the 1960s, gradually giving way to new trends in the early 1970s.

Leading British artist Bridget Riley stands in front of one of her works in the 1960s Op art style, of which she was a pioneer. Op stood for 'optical', referring to the illusion of vibrating movement experienced by a viewer when looking at this kind of picture. Op art had a strong influence, not only on art but on 1960s fashions in clothes.

What the papers said

The paintings appear to be uncompromisingly faithful to detail. Mr Warhol's painting *Turkey Vegetable*, for example, is the twin of his equally honest *Chicken Noodle*, except for the words 'turkey vegetable' and 'chicken noodle'. The total effect, I thought, was one of seeing perhaps more paintings of soup cans than one might care to see. I suspected for a moment, even, that Mr Warhol might have had his tongue in his cheek.... I took a final look at Warhol's *Consomme*. I noticed the first 'm' was larger than the second.... Perhaps, I mused, Warhol had been trying to tell us something there.

Jack Smith in the *Los Angeles Times*, 23 July 1962

- **SEE ALSO**
Pages 18–19: 8 February 1964: Beatlemania Hits the USA

Pages 38–39: 15 August 1969: The First Day at Woodstock

- **FURTHER INFORMATION**
  📖 Books:
  Pop Art by Richard Spilsbury (Heinemann, 2009)
  🖱 Websites:
  www.popartists.com
  A gallery of pop artists

22 OCTOBER 1962

The Cuban Missile Crisis

A frightening episode in the Cold War began on Monday 22 October 1962, when US President John F Kennedy made a broadcast to the American people. He told them that the USA was under threat from nearby Cuba. Soviet teams on the island were secretly constructing nuclear missile sites, and the missiles themselves were being brought to Cuba by Soviet vessels. Kennedy announced a US 'quarantine' – in effect, a blockade of Cuba. Any ships carrying armaments would be turned back by the US Navy. As 25 Soviet vessels were heading for Cuba, it seemed likely that they would refuse to submit to a search. And if that led to an armed clash, it might trigger a nuclear war.

Cuba under Castro

The origins of the crisis lay in the American–Cuban hostility that developed after Fidel Castro and his followers took power on the island in January 1959. Having ousted a corrupt dictatorship, Castro introduced a number of reforms, some of which injured American economic interests. An American-backed attempt to overthrow Castro failed humiliatingly, and American anger increased as Cuba became closely allied with its Cold War adversary, the Soviet Union.

To Americans, establishing nuclear bases on Cuba was an intolerable threat. From the Soviet point of view, protecting an endangered ally was legitimate, and nuclear sites on Cuba were no different from the US bases established near the Soviet bloc, including those recently established on the Soviet frontier with Turkey.

Khrushchev and Kennedy

However, both the Soviet leader, Nikita Khrushchev, and President Kennedy realized that the two sides had so many weapons that a nuclear war would wreck the planet and possibly destroy the human race. They wanted to avoid war, but without backing down. On 24 October, some

The closest of allies: Cuban leader Fidel Castro and the Soviet Union's Khrushchev embrace on meeting for the first time in 1960 at the United Nations General Assembly.

Cuba-bound ships turned back, while the US allowed other vessels through without searching them. But work on the missile sites went on, and an American invasion of Cuba seemed imminent.

Then, on the 27th and 28th, an exchange of messages led to an agreement. The Soviet sites would be dismantled in return for an American promise not to attack Cuba. Secretly, Kennedy also promised to remove US bases in Turkey. Since this was not known, Kennedy appeared to have stood firm and was hailed in the West as a hero. In fact, Kennedy and Khrushchev had together – against the wishes of some of their close advisers – saved the world from catastrophe.

Exit strategy: the US blockade of Cuba ended when the Soviets agreed to remove their missiles from the island. But US ships continued to monitor the situation. Here, the USS Barry (foreground) steams alongside the Soviet freighter Ansov, which has left Cuba laden with military hardware.

What the papers said

Last night's grim speech [by President Kennedy] was a new turn in the Kennedy–Khrushchev relationship, a calculated risk and one full of danger. But the President saw no acceptable alternative because, as he said, 'the greatest danger of all would be to do nothing'.... Certainly in the nuclear war that the President spoke of last night as a possibility 'even the fruits of a victory would be ashes in our mouths'. But there are times in history when men and nations must act. The President has judged this as such a moment.

The Washington Post, 23 October 1962

- **SEE ALSO**
  Pages 8–9: 13 August 1961:
  The Berlin Wall Rises
  Pages 32–33: 20 August 1968:
  Soviet Forces Invade Czechoslovakia

- **FURTHER INFORMATION**
  Books:
  Kennedy and the Cuban Missile Crisis
  by Cath Senker (Raintree, 2013)
  Websites:
  library.thinkquest.org/11046
  Fourteen Days in October: the Cuban Missile
  Crisis – an interactive site

The 'I Have a Dream' Speech

Over 200,000 marchers, black and white, assembled in the US capital, Washington, DC, to demand full civil rights for black people. A leading campaigner, Martin Luther King, Jr, made a speech from the steps of the Lincoln Memorial that has never been forgotten. In the rhythmic tones of a preacher, he said, again and again, 'I have a dream'. The dream was one in which black and white would live together in equality and brotherhood, with all hatred and bitterness put aside. He ended with a vision of all humanity 'free at last!'

Slavery and segregation

Martin Luther King makes his famous 'I have a dream' speech in front of the Lincoln Memorial, Washington, DC, at the end of the Freedom March for racial equality.

Black people had often been treated badly in the USA. The ancestors of America's black population had come to the country as slaves, taken by force from their African homes. Concentrated in the South (now the south-eastern region of the USA), they became free only when President Abraham Lincoln abolished slavery during the Civil War of 1861–1865.

However, their freedom was limited in practice, because the southern states passed local laws designed to hold them down. It was made as difficult as possible for blacks to become registered voters, let alone hold public office. Whites had priority in jobs and housing, and a policy of segregation forced blacks to use separate and usually inferior schools, transport facilities and eating places.

Civil rights

Things began to change in December 1955 after a black woman named Rosa Parks refused to give up her seat on a bus to a white man in Montgomery, Alabama. Parks was fined, but the incident ignited a determined civil rights movement. As it gathered strength, a Baptist minister, Martin Luther King, emerged as its most effective leader. King preached, and practised, non-violent action, although he and his followers in southern states faced arrests, beatings and, in some instances, killings.

The August 1963 demonstration, and King's speech, impressed the world and led to the 1964 Civil Rights Act, which showed a new resolve to end segregation and other injustices. King remained in the forefront of the movement and was awarded the Nobel Peace Prize in 1964, but in 1968 he was shot dead. By that time, the civil rights battle was almost won, although it would be 40 years until Barack Obama became the first black president. Also, poverty remained an issue for blacks in the South and in the slums of the northern cities.

Moved and inspired, Martin Luther King's fellow marchers cheer his speech. Heard by some 200,000 people in Washington, DC, King's 'dream' made a great impact at the time. It was reported in newspapers and seen on film and television and it is now regarded as a classic statement of human aspirations.

What the papers said

The national conscience … has been stirred…. The only question is whether the translation of attitude into action will come fast enough to prevent new explosions of interracial violence. The unity of Negro and white citizens in the leadership of the march and in its rank and file demonstrated the indivisibility of the fight for genuine equality in all phases of American affairs. It was a rebuke to those in both races … who favour a pulling-apart instead of a pulling-together.

The New York Times, 30 August 1963

- **FURTHER INFORMATION**
- 📖 Books:
  Martin Luther King Jr. by Wil Mara (Children's Press, 2013)
- Websites:
  www.seattletimes.com/special/mlk
  Martin Luther King, Jr and the civil rights movement

The President is Assassinated

It happened at about 12.30 pm, as the motorcade moved slowly through the streets of Dallas, the second largest city in the state of Texas. Behind the first car and police motorcyclists, a dark blue, open-topped Lincoln automobile drove at 11 miles per hour through streets lined with armed police and cheering people. Inside the Lincoln sat Texas governor John Connally and his wife. The back seats held the guests of honour, President John F Kennedy and his wife Jackie, newly arrived in the city on the second day of a visit to Texas.

Kennedy is shot

The couple were waving to the crowd when shots were heard. The president fell forward, crying 'My God, I'm hit!', and clutched his throat. Governor Connally, also hit, was covered in blood. Then there was another shot, and Kennedy was flung backwards. The bullet had blown a hole in his head, and Jackie Kennedy screamed as blood and brain tissue spattered the compartment. The president fell into his wife's arms as the Lincoln accelerated. Now leading the motorcade, it raced to the nearby Parkland Memorial Hospital. Despite emergency surgery, the president was pronounced dead at 1 pm.

President Kennedy and his wife Jackie smile at the crowds lining the streets of Dallas to greet them. Minutes later, despite the heavy security around the motorcade, shots rang out and an assassin's bullets mortally wounded the president.

The likely assassin

Reports suggested that the shots were fired from one of the tall buildings lining the route, a schoolbook warehouse. Among its employees was Lee Harvey Oswald, a young man whose erratic past included a period living in the Soviet Union. Pursued, Oswald took refuge in a cinema, where he was arrested. He protested his innocence, but on 24 November, before the investigation had got very far, he was shot dead while being transferred to the county gaol. The killer, a nightclub owner named Jack Ruby, claimed to have acted to avenge Jackie Kennedy.

24 November 1963, Dallas police station: Jack Ruby shoots Lee Harvey Oswald, the alleged assassin of President Kennedy.

A conspiracy?

There was convincing evidence to link Oswald with the rifle and cartridges found on the sixth floor of the warehouse, and in 1964 the specially appointed Warren Commission concluded that he had acted alone. But many contradictory facts remained unaccounted for, and later investigators believed that there might have been more than one gunman acting as part of a conspiracy, rather than a single, presumably unhinged individual. One plausible theory blamed the Mafia, a powerful criminal organization that was under investigation by Kennedy's administration. However, it now seems unlikely that the full story behind Kennedy's death will ever be known.

What the papers said

Word of President Kennedy's assassination struck the world's capitals with shattering impact, leaving heads of state and the man in the street stunned and grief-stricken…. Pubs in London and cafes in Paris fell silent, as the news came over radio and television. In Moscow, a Russian girl walked weeping along the street. At UN headquarters in New York, delegates of 11 nations bowed their heads in a moment of silence. In Buenos Aires, newspapers sounded sirens reserved for news of the utmost gravity…. Sir Winston Churchill branded the slaying a monstrous act.

The Dallas Morning News, 23 November 1963

- **SEE ALSO**
  Pages 12–13: 22 October 1962: The Cuban Missile Crisis

- **FURTHER INFORMATION**
  Books:
  Presidential Biographies: John F. Kennedy by Erin Edison (Capstone, 2012)
  Websites:
  www.jfklibrary.org
  John F. Kennedy's life and place in history

Beatlemania Hits the USA

After the plane touched down at Kennedy Airport in New York, fans broke through the police cordon and thousands fought to see the Beatles. No other British pop group had received such a reception in the USA. Over the next fortnight, the Beatles were pursued, and were often in danger of being mobbed, at every stage of their visit. Their US triumph confirmed that they were not merely stars in Britain and Europe, but had become a worldwide phenomenon.

Four young men

The Beatles were four young men from Liverpool – John Lennon, Paul McCartney, George Harrison and Ringo Starr. Most of the group had worked together since the late 1950s, but they had become the Beatles only in 1960. Their distinctive image – brushed-forward hair and neat 'mod' suits – was even more recent, dating from shortly before their first recording in 1962, *Love Me Do*. This was moderately successful, but their next single, *Please Please Me*, reached number one in the UK charts, and one hit followed another in the course of 1963. Beatlemania swept Britain, and in November the Beatles appeared at the Royal Variety Performance.

The Beatles arrive at Kennedy Airport and get a foretaste of the welcome they will receive everywhere in the USA. Waving and smiling, they are (left to right) John Lennon, Paul McCartney, George Harrison (guitars) and Ringo Starr (drums).

A new sound

Liverpool was a major centre of rock music in the 1960s, and other successful Liverpudlian groups included Gerry and the Pacemakers and the Searchers. But the Beatles made an incomparable impression. At this time their songs, many written by the Lennon-McCartney partnership, were in the heavy 'Merseybeat' style, but with some individual touches and with distinctive high 'oohs' that became a Beatles trademark.

Their group personality was a significant part of the Beatles' impact. They were young, working class and cheekily irreverent without being really offensive. Seemingly ordinary, they appealed to the youth culture that was such a feature of the 1960s. Their success in the USA was the start of a cult of Britishness, when 'swinging London' became the centre of youth fashion, with miniskirts by Mary Quant, and Carnaby Street the place to buy trendy clothes.

Later years

The Beatles proved to have unusual musical talents. Lennon and McCartney, and later George Harrison, composed many strikingly original songs, notably for the 1967 album *Sgt. Pepper's Lonely Hearts Club Band*. They remained responsive to the popular mood, adopting much of the hippy outlook of the later 1960s. In 1970 the Beatles broke up, but remained individually active. John Lennon was assassinated in New York in 1980. George Harrison died of cancer in 2001.

American teenagers scream with emotion during a performance by the Beatles at the Coliseum, Washington, DC, in February 1964.

What the papers said

About 500 teenagers, most of them girls, had shown up at the Plaza [Hotel].... One group of girls asked everybody who came out, 'Did you see the Beatles? Did you touch them?' A policeman came up, and one of them yelled, 'He touched a Beatle! I saw him!' The girls jumped on the cop's arms and back, but it wasn't a mob assault. There were goony smiles all over their faces.
Tom Wolfe, *New York Herald Tribune*, 8 February 1964

• SEE ALSO
Pages 38–39: 15 August 1969: The First Day at Woodstock

• FURTHER INFORMATION
Books:
The Beatles: British Pop Sensation by Stuart A. Kallen (Greenhaven Press, 2011)
Websites:
www.beatles.com
The Beatles' official website

The Marines Arrive in Vietnam

Two battalions of US Marines waded ashore at Da Nang in South Vietnam, where the US air base had to be protected against guerrilla fighters. There were only 3,500 marines, but they were the first contingent of American combat troops to be sent to Vietnam. In June they saw action for the first time and by the end of 1965 another 18,000 troops had landed. The USA had become deeply involved in a South-East Asian conflict that, despite its military might, it would fail to win.

Marines come ashore from landing craft at Da Nang. Their arrival marked the beginning of an increasingly costly and demoralizing US involvement in the South Vietnam conflict.

Divided country

Vietnam was a French colony until 1954, when it was divided into a communist northern state, led by Ho Chi Minh, and anti-communist South Vietnam. Determined to prevent the spread of communism, the USA supported the South Vietnamese dictator Ngo Dinh Diem. A resistance movement, the National Liberation Front for South Vietnam (NLF), became active in the south during the early 1960s, supplied by North Vietnam down the 'Ho Chi Minh trail' – well-concealed jungle paths along the frontiers of neighbouring Cambodia and Laos. President Kennedy stepped up the American effort, sending substantial aid and increasing the US presence to 15,000 'advisers' to prop up the South Vietnamese army.

Deepening conflict

Under Kennedy's successor, Lyndon B Johnson, the USA became even more deeply involved. In 1964, the USA began a devastating bombing campaign against North Vietnam, followed by the landing of the marines in 1965. The USA's direct involvement in the war ultimately drew in over half a million Americans. The NLF's jungle hideouts gave them some protection, but US bombs, shells and napalm took a heavy toll.

Despite US help, South Vietnam's forces performed badly. The USA carried a heavy burden and by the end of the conflict had lost 58,000 men. By 1967, more and more Americans were joining anti-war protests, leading to bitter divisions among Americans.

Withdrawal and defeat

The turning point was the January 1968 Tet Offensive, when the NLF for a time held South Vietnamese cities and penetrated into the heart of the capital, Saigon. President Johnson refused requests to send more troops and, soon afterwards, started peace talks with North Vietnam. The violence was far from over, but US forces withdrew between 1969 and 1973, leaving a supposedly reinvigorated and re-equipped South Vietnamese army to carry on. They failed to stop the resistance, and in 1975 North Vietnam conquered the South, ending the Vietnam War.

Civilians flee from the fighting in Saigon during the Tet Offensive launched by the NLF in May 1968.

◉ eye witness

I was walking in a single file of Vietnamese soldiers along the narrow banks that divided the paddy fields of the Mekong delta.... When the shell burst, my impression was that a small volcano had sprung out of the ground.... I felt a tremendous shudder through the soles of my boots, and then the blast threw me to the ground.... My heart thumped and my hands shook. Then I heard a half sob, half gasp.... it was my friend from Nha Trang, clasping his stomach.... He was dying.

Gavin Young, *Slow Boats to China* (Hutchinson, 1981)

- **SEE ALSO**
  Pages 30–31: 10 May 1968: The Barricades Rise in Paris

- **FURTHER INFORMATION**
  📖 Books:
  Living Through the Vietnam War by Cath Senker (Raintree, 2012)
  🖱 Websites:
  http://www.spartacus.schoolnet.co.uk/vietnam.html
  Main figures, events, issues and organizations

The Cultural Revolution Erupts

After months of political manoeuvres, debates and demonstrations, it was official. On 8 August 1966, the Central Committee of the Chinese Communist Party proclaimed the '16 points' of a programme that would guide the Great Proletarian Cultural Revolution.

Mao Zedong

The driving force behind the Cultural Revolution was the legendary Mao Zedong, under whose leadership the Communist Party had seized power in 1949. Now in his 70s, Mao was revered but had lost political influence during the 1960s. The Cultural Revolution involved, among other things, Mao's return to power and the elimination of hostile factions within the government. But Mao also genuinely believed that China's ruling Communist Party had lost much of its revolutionary fervour and was becoming a privileged elite. Moreover, old pre-communist values were still lingering, so mass action was needed to root out 'the four olds' – old ideas, old culture, old customs, old habits.

● eye witness

I saw a dozen or so teachers standing on the platform on the sports ground, with their heads bent and their arms twisted [behind them].... some were kicked on the back of their knees and forced to kneel, while others, including my English-language teacher, an elderly man ... were forced to stand on long, narrow benches. He ... swayed and fell, cutting his forehead on the sharp corner of a bench. A Red Guard standing next to him instinctively stooped and extended his hand to help, but immediately straightened up ... yelling: 'Get back onto the bench!' He did not want to be seen as soft.

Jung Chang describes a 'denunciation meeting' during her schooldays in *Wild Swans* (Flamingo, 1993)

Red Guards

To achieve his aims, Mao looked for help to the army, led by his ally Lin Piao, and to the millions of Chinese students, organized into militant Red Guards. Flourishing the famous 'Little Red Book' of Chairman Mao's thoughts, the Red Guards moved through the country, denouncing and humiliating officials, teachers, writers and artists. Huge numbers of people were exiled to the countryside to be 're-educated' by hard work.

Red Guards destroyed many 'old' works of art, and schools, universities, temples and churches were closed. In some places Red Guards set up committees as rivals to the existing authorities. Where officials resisted, a

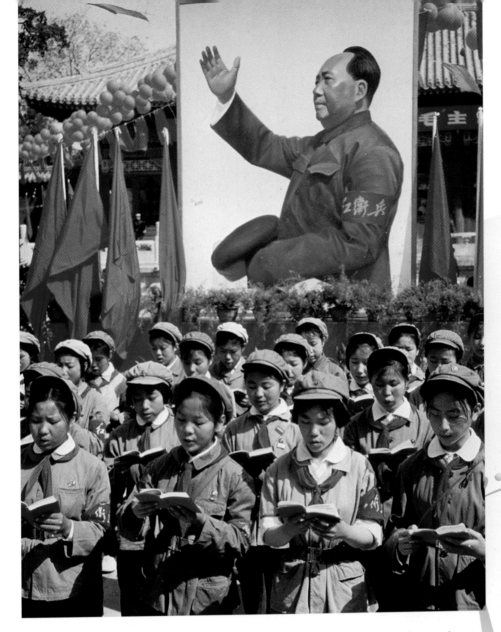

Standing in front of a picture of Mao, young Chinese read from their copies of the 'Little Red Book' of Mao's sayings, the approved text for aspiring Cultural Revolutionaries.

situation close to civil war developed. The Red Guards themselves split into factions and fought one another.

Chaos and disaster

By 1968 the situation in China was so chaotic that Mao called a halt to the Cultural Revolution, without admitting that it had been a disaster. The Cultural Revolution was said to have achieved its aims, which was true only in that Mao had removed all his leading rivals. Mao's chosen successor, army chief Lin Piao, was the next to go, killed in a plane crash in 1971 while fleeing after a failed coup attempt. The Cultural Revolution caused immense suffering and its effects on Chinese society and its economy lasted for many years. Mao remained in charge until his death in 1976, after which new leaders set China on a radically different course.

FURTHER INFORMATION

Books:
The Chinese Cultural Revolution by Louise Chipley Slavicek (Chelsea House Publishers, 2010)

Websites:
www.historylearningsite.co.uk/cultural_revolution.htm
The Cultural Revolution

30
MAY
1967

Biafra Breaks Away from Nigeria

The Republic of Biafra was born on 30 May 1967. Colonel Odumegwu Ojukwu, military governor of Nigeria's Eastern Region, declared that the region had become the sovereign state of Biafra and no longer owed allegiance to Nigeria. The Nigerian ruler, Colonel Yakubu Gowon, denounced the breakaway and predicted that it would be short-lived.

Military coups

A large and heavily populated country in West Africa, Nigeria had been a British colony until 1960. It was a land of widely different peoples, and old antagonisms surfaced when Nigeria ran into economic problems. In January 1966 an army coup overthrew its notoriously corrupt civilian government. The new military regime was dominated by officers belonging to the Ibo people, but in July 1966 it was overthrown by a rival army faction, mostly from the northern tribes, which made Colonel Gowon head of state.

Massacres

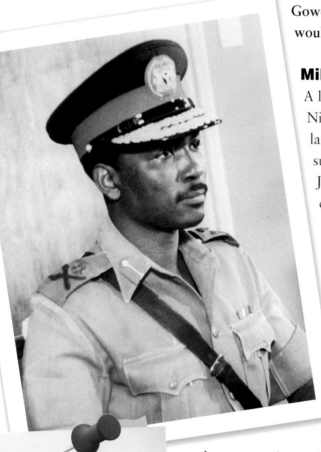

Yakubu Gowon, head of Nigeria's military government at the time of Biafra's attempt to break away and become independent.

Two months later there was unrest in the north, and savage attacks were made on the Ibos. Their homeland was in the Eastern Region, but large numbers had emigrated to other parts of Nigeria. Like immigrants in many countries, the Ibos were often unpopular, and the attacks on them turned into large-scale massacres. An estimated 30,000 Ibos were killed, and half a million of them fled back to the Eastern Region.

Gowon had done little to stop the massacres, adding to the Ibos' fears. When he published plans for territorial changes unfavourable to the Ibos, Ojukwu proclaimed an independent Biafra. Although relatively small, Biafra did have the advantage of being rich in oil. This was Nigeria's major natural resource, so Gowon's government was quite determined not to accept the breakaway.

Learning to use a rifle: a training camp at Owerri for young Biafran soldiers. After initial instruction, the young men went straight to the front to fight with increasing desperation against Nigerian government forces.

War

War broke out on 6 July 1967. Unexpectedly, the Biafrans took the initiative and advanced into the neighbouring territory. But weight of numbers soon began to tell, and the Nigerian government forces slowly drove back the Biafrans. When Port Harcourt fell in May 1968, Biafra lost its access to the sea and the Shell oil refineries. The war was lost, but the Biafrans fought on stubbornly for 18 months, eventually supplied by only a single airstrip. Though heroic, their efforts brought immense suffering to the Ibo people, at least half a million of whom died from starvation.

Finally, after two and a half years of war, Biafra surrendered in January 1970. Nigeria was reunited, but endured continuing political instability during the late 20th century.

What the papers said

In Enugu there was dancing in the streets and chanting by massed crowds as the Ojukwu regime went through with the full ceremonies for the proclamation of a new state…. The new Biafran flag – red, black and green with a rising sun device – was hoisted to the accompaniment of a 42-gun salute. Crowds, predominantly Ibos, carried the tree branches that symbolized an occasion of national rejoicing, and shouted: 'Biafra, Biafra, we hail thee. Nigeria is dead. We are Biafrans now.'

Guardian, 31 May 1967

- **SEE ALSO**
  Pages 4–5: 21 March 1960:
  Massacre at Sharpeville
  Pages 6–7: 30 June 1960:
  The Congo Gains its Independence

- **FURTHER INFORMATION**
  📖 Books:
  Nigeria by Ida Walker
  (Mason Crest Publishers, 2013)
  Websites:
  www.factmonster.com/ipka/A0107847.html
  History of Nigeria

05 JUNE 1967

Israeli Strikes Launch the Six-Day War

At 8.45 am, Egyptian time, Israeli aircraft struck hard at Egypt's airfields. They achieved complete surprise. Wave after wave of planes followed, relentlessly bombing and strafing the Egyptian airfields and then returning to their bases. There, they were refuelled, reloaded and sent back into action so rapidly that Egyptian observers believed the Israelis must be receiving help from other air forces. Most Egyptian planes were destroyed on the ground, but some managed to take off, only to be shot down in dogfights. Within three hours the main onslaught was over. The Egyptians had lost almost 300 aircraft.

Israel's victory

In one day of fighting, Israel had established an overwhelming superiority in the air that would give it a decisive advantage in the war that followed. Meanwhile, Israeli ground forces had attacked Egyptian positions in Gaza and the Sinai Peninsula. Israeli hopes of taking on only a single opponent were dashed when Jordan, Syria and Iraq declared war. However, Israeli forces won decisive victories and occupied Gaza, the Sinai Peninsula, the West

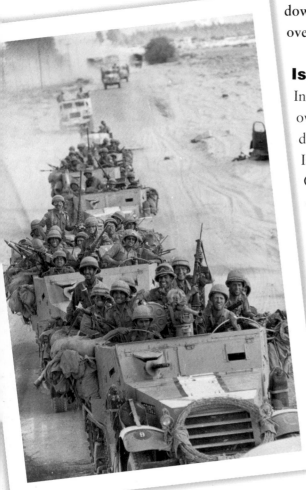

Triumphant offensive: Israeli armour surges into Egypt during the Six-Day War.

 eye witness

There must be at least 10,000 vehicles abandoned in Sinai; some are total wrecks, others untouched…. In the Mitla Pass two miles of vehicles, soft-skinned and armoured, nose to tail, had been wrecked and wrecked again by air attack. Other convoys lay like broken-backed snakes across the desert roads. At other times it was like flying over a table exercise [war game], with whole tank squadrons in formation knocked out…. Claims of 500 tanks knocked out must be valid and may be an underestimate.

Charles Douglas-Home in *The Times*, 11 June 1967

Desperate flight: though this bridge has been wrecked, Palestinian refugees from the West Bank make their way across it to reach Jordan during the Six-Day War.

Bank and East Jerusalem. Finally, they stormed the Golan Heights, an area of southern Syria that had long been used to bombard Israeli settlements on the other side of the frontier.

An ongoing conflict

In six days, Israel had changed the map of the Middle East. But the problems that had caused the war had not gone away. The conflict began when increasing Jewish settlement in Palestine in the early 20th century aroused Arab antagonism. In 1948 Palestine was partitioned and the Jewish state of Israel was set up. Israel was attacked by the neighbouring Arab states, but survived.

Meanwhile, many thousands of Palestinian Arabs fled or were driven from their homes. They became refugees, living in camps in neighbouring states or the parts of Palestine held by Arab states – Gaza by Egypt, East Jerusalem and the West Bank by Jordan.

The situation remained unchanged after a second war in 1956. Then in 1967 Israel again seemed threatened by its neighbours and decided to strike first. Israel's victory brought many Palestinians under its rule, a fact that complicated rather than resolved the conflict. The Arab–Israeli issue was still troubling the world in the 21st century.

- **FURTHER INFORMATION**
  - **Books:**
    The Arab-Israeli Conflict
    by Nicola Barber (Rosen Central, 2012)
  - **Websites:**
    http://news.bbc.co.uk/onthisday/hi/dates/stories
    /june/10/newsid_3047000/3047177.stm
    Memories of the 1967 Arab-Israeli War

The First Human Heart Transplant

Louis Washkansky, a 55-year-old South African grocer, suffered from diabetes and an incurable heart condition that was certain to kill him within weeks. His only chance was to undergo an operation that had never yet been performed: the removal of his diseased heart and its replacement by a healthy organ.

A daunting challenge

The obstacles were formidable. The replacement could only come from a dead person whose heart was still beating. And as the heart deteriorates rapidly after death, the operation would have to be carried out very quickly. A further problem was that the human immune system rejects

Dr Christiaan Barnard shows an X-ray image of his patient Louis Washkansky's chest, taken during the first heart transplant operation.

foreign materials. However, the heart of a young woman who had been killed in an automobile accident became available, and the chances of success were increased by the fact that she had the same blood-group as Washkansky. The odds were further improved by the use of drugs that weakened the patient's immune system.

The operation

The operation was carried out by Dr Christiaan Barnard and a team of 20 surgeons at the Groote Schuur Hospital in Cape Town, South Africa. It lasted for five hours. Most of Washkansky's heart was removed and he was kept alive by a heart-lung machine, which took over the function of the removed organ, oxygenating the blood and pumping it into the main arteries. Then the donor heart was sewn onto the connective tissues. It was smaller than the organ it replaced, which meant that it would have to work harder to do its job. The critical moment came when Barnard applied electrodes to the new heart, shocking it into a regular beat. Washkansky was going to survive.

The operation created a worldwide sensation, but its real success was limited. Because of the drugs that suppressed Washkansky's immune system, he was unable to fight off infections. Eighteen days after the operation, he died of pneumonia. Barnard's second transplant patient, Philip Blaiberg, lived for 19 months, but in general survival rates were poor.

eye witness

A 20-joule charge of [electricity] … shot through the squirming muscles, causing the body of Louis Washkansky to arch upward as though kicked in the back. For a moment the heart lay paralysed, without any sign of life. We waited – it seemed like hours – until it slowly began to relax. Then it came like a bolt of light. There was a sudden contraction of the atria, followed quickly by the ventricles in obedient response – then the atria, and again the ventricles. Little by little it began to roll with the lovely rhythm of life, the heartbeat of the world.

Christiaan Barnard recalls the operation in One Life *(George G. Harrap & Co Ltd, 1970)*

Progress

For a time it looked as though heart transplants were more spectacular than useful. But the development of the immunosuppressant cyclosporine, and other improvements in treatment, transformed patients' chances of living for years rather than months. In 1981, the success of a triple transplant – heart, liver and lungs – demonstrated the immense advances made by medical science and confirmed Christiaan Barnard's place in medical history.

- **FURTHER INFORMATION**
- 📖 **Books:**
  What are the Limits of Organ Transplants?
  by Anna Claybourne
  (Raintree, 2012)
- Ⓦ **Websites:**
  www.cbsnews.com/htdocs/transplants/
  timeline.html
  A timeline of transplant history

Barricades Rise in Paris

After days of violent clashes between students and police, on 10 May students prepared to defend the Latin Quarter, site of Paris's ancient university, the Sorbonne. They threw up 60 barricades, made with piled-up paving stones and upturned vehicles. At around 2.15 am, riot police attacked with truncheons, tear gas and stun grenades, while the students sheltered behind the barricades and flung paving stones and some home-made petrol bombs.

Strikes and protests

Not for the first time, the police acted with an extreme brutality that united students and local residents against them. There were protests all over France, and on 13 May a one-day general strike took place. Around 800,000 people marched through Paris, calling for an end to General Charles de Gaulle's ten-year rule. Soon the students had occupied the Sorbonne, and millions of workers went on strike, taking over their factories and offices. France seemed to be on the verge of revolution.

In reality, there was no plan to take power. People began to tire of endless disruption, and concessions to the workers and students weakened their ardour. On 16 June the 200 students left in the Sorbonne were evicted by the police. On 30 June, de Gaulle's supporters won a landslide victory in a general election.

May 1968: Parisian students fling stones at the riot police during a period of violent clashes. For a time it seemed as though France was on the brink of revolution.

Student movements

France's 'student revolt' was not an isolated event. Militancy among young people, especially students, was widespread in the 1960s, starting with black and white US students who took part in the struggle for civil rights. Most student movements began with specific grievances about campus restrictions or teaching. A minority held radical political views, mainly of a 'New Left' type – socialist and would-be revolutionary, but opposed to the rigid, oppressive socialism associated with Soviet communism. In France, New Leftists like Daniel Cohn-Bendit, known as 'Danny the Red', became increasingly prominent as the student movement became radicalized.

The New Left owed much of its short-lived influence to the Vietnam War. More than any other issue, this turned students to militancy, starting in the USA at Berkeley, California, in 1964. Student unrest spread to the universities and art colleges of Britain, to France, West Germany and Italy. Everywhere students used similar disruptive tactics – sit-ins (occupation of university buildings) and teach-ins (debates), as well as demonstrations and marches. Student movements went on into the early 1970s before fading away, their more ambitious hopes unfulfilled.

The evacuation of the Sorbonne by police in June 1968. Some students left of their own accord. Others had to be removed by force.

eye witness

It was astounding to watch the students being unafraid of police with tear gas and CS gas, concussion grenades, nightsticks, pistols, helmets, visors, shields, grenade rifles, and the famous leaded capes. It was equally astounding to find their courage 'rewarded', so to speak, by sympathy and even admiration ... from the public at large. The fight was so unequal, the police so brutal that you had to be a very determined Law and Order person to feel sympathy for the authorities.

Hans Koning Nineteen Sixty Eight: A Personal Report *(Unwin Hyman, 1988)*

- **SEE ALSO**
  Pages 14–15: 28 August 1963:
  The 'I Have a Dream' Speech
  Pages 20–21: 8 March 1965:
  The Marines Arrive in Vietnam

- **FURTHER INFORMATION**
  Websites:
  http://news.bbc.co.uk/onthisday/hi/dates/stories
  /may/13/newsid_2512000/2512413.stm
  Paris student protests

Soviet Forces Invade Czechoslovakia

The invasion began on the night of 20 August. Most Czechoslovaks realized what had happened only when they awoke the next morning and saw Soviet tanks in the streets. The Soviets and their allies claimed that they had been invited in to protect the country, but this was soon shown to be a lie. The main Czech authorities refused to be cowed and denounced the occupation. And although armed resistance would have been futile against the overwhelming strength of the invaders, ordinary people made their furious feelings clear, the boldest actually climbing onto tanks and arguing with their crews. The Soviets quickly tightened their grip, taking over the government and media and arresting the Czech leader, Alexander Dubcek.

May 1968, before the storm: Czech leader Alexander Dubcek is greeted with joy by supporters of his reform programme. Talks with the Soviet leadership appeared to have succeeded, but three months later the Soviets invaded.

The Prague Spring

The invasion ended an exciting experiment. Czechoslovakia was a communist state and one of the East European allies of the Soviet Union. (Since 1992, Czechoslovakia has been replaced by two states, the Czech and Slovak republics.) The communist states had socialist systems in which the entire economy was run by the state, supposedly for the benefit of the people. But any advantages the system may have had were outweighed by the dominant role played by the Communist Party and the lack of political rights and freedom of speech, which had led to terrible abuses.

Dubcek became the Czech leader in January 1968 and by April he had launched a full-scale reform programme. Censorship was lifted, past crimes were investigated and basic freedoms began to be established. This was to be 'socialism with a human face'. Delighted Czechs called it the Prague Spring.

The Soviet response

Dubcek knew that his programme would alarm the Soviet Union and he repeatedly insisted on his loyalty to the Soviet-led military alliance, the Warsaw Pact. Yet he underestimated the Soviet leaders' fear that Czech reforms might inspire calls for change in other communist regimes. After months of fruitless high-level meetings and thinly veiled threats, the Soviets and their Warsaw Pact allies acted.

The strong reaction against the invasion persuaded the Soviets to move cautiously. Dubcek was allowed to stay in office and hoped to carry out at least some reforms. However, the balance of power within the Czech Communist Party gradually shifted, and in April 1969 Dubcek was forced out. Under his successor, Gustav Husak, the Czechoslovakian government returned to the oppressive ways of the previous regime and the idea of reforming communism was shelved indefinitely.

Unable to resist the might of the invading Warsaw Pact forces, Czechs nevertheless made it clear that they were outraged. In the capital, Prague, this young man is risking his life by climbing onto a Soviet T-54 tank.

⊙ eye witness

It was almost 9.00 am when about eight Soviet paratroopers and one or two lower officers burst into my office and closed and blocked the windows and connecting doors. It was like an armed robbery … the main door flew open again and in walked some higher officers of the KGB, including a highly decorated, very short colonel … [who] told us that he was taking us 'under his protection'. Indeed we were protected, sitting around that table – each of us had a tommy gun pointed at the back of his head.

Alexander Dubcek's memories of the morning he was arrested, recalled in *Hope Dies Last* (Harper Collins, 1993)

- **SEE ALSO**
  Pages 8–9: 13 August 1961:
  The Berlin Wall Rises
  Pages 12–13: 22 October 1962:
  The Cuban Missiles Crisis

- **FURTHER INFORMATION**
  📖 Books:
  The Cold War
  by R. G. Grant (Arcturus, 2011)
  🖱 Websites:
  www.coldwar.org
  The Cold War Museum

The First Men on the Moon

On 20 July 1969, a lunar module carried Neil Armstrong and Edwin 'Buzz' Aldrin down from their spacecraft, Apollo 11, to the surface of the Moon. From the module, nicknamed the Eagle, Armstrong sent Mission Control at Houston, Texas, the first-ever message from the surface: 'Houston, Tranquillity Base here. The Eagle has landed.' After the astronauts had strapped on their backpacks, Armstrong opened a door, came out of it backwards, and climbed down a ladder. He turned on the lunar module's TV camera and then became the first man to set foot on the Moon. Back on Earth, 600 million people watched the event on their TV sets and heard Armstrong declare, 'That's one small step for a man, one giant leap for mankind.'

Apollo 11

This was the high point of a voyage that began on 16 July, when Apollo 11 left Cape Canaveral, Florida, looking small by comparison with the Saturn rocket on which it rode. The fuel and liquid oxygen in the rocket blasted Apollo out of the Earth's atmosphere. As each step of its job was done, part of the rocket fell away, finally leaving just the Apollo 11 spacecraft to complete the journey.

The spacecraft was made up of three parts: the command module, where the astronauts lived; the service module, which contained the engines and other systems; and the lunar module, which would make the Moon landing. As they approached their target, the astronauts manoeuvred Apollo into orbit 111 kilometres above the Moon; Michael Collins remained on board while Armstrong and Aldrin made their historic descent in the lunar module.

An historic moment: Apollo 11 is launched from pad 39A at Kennedy Space Center, Florida, on 16 July 1969. Four days later, Neil Armstrong and Edwin 'Buzz' Aldrin became the first men to set foot on the Moon.

They spent only a short time on the surface, setting up a memorial and carrying out scientific work, before going back to Apollo 11 for the return journey. On 24 July the command module splashed down in the Pacific with the three astronauts on board.

The space race

This great achievement received much of its impetus from the Cold War rivalry between the USA and the Soviet Union. In April 1961 the world was astonished to learn that a Soviet army officer, Yuri Gagarin, had become the first man in space. President Kennedy responded by declaring that the USA would put a man on the Moon by the end of the decade. After huge efforts and many rehearsals, the goal was achieved. Five more manned Moon landings were made up to 1975, after which the emphasis shifted to unmanned flights, further and further out into space.

Walking on the surface of the Moon: Buzz Aldrin steps out at Tranquillity Base, in a photograph taken by fellow astronaut Neil Armstrong.

⊙ eye witness

Of all the spectacular views we had, the most impressive to me was on the way to the Moon, when we flew through its shadow. We were still thousands of miles away, but ... the Moon almost filled our circular window. It was eclipsing the Sun ... and the corona of the Sun was visible around the limb of the Moon as a gigantic lens-shaped or saucer-shaped light, stretching out to several lunar diameters. It was magnificent, but the Moon was even more so ... no part of it illuminated by the Sun. It was illuminated only by earthshine.

Neil Armstrong recalls a magic moment in First on the Moon: a Voyage with Neil Armstrong, Michael Collins, Edwin E. Aldrin Jr, *written with Gene Farmer and Dora Jane Hamblin (Michael Joseph, 1970)*

- **FURTHER INFORMATION**
📖 Books:
   Moon Landing: Apollo 11 40th Anniversary Pop-Up by Richard Platt (Candlewick, 2008)
🖰 Websites:
   www.nasa.gov
   NASA's official website

British Troops Arrive in Northern Ireland

British forces were sent to Northern Ireland as a temporary measure, to restore order. Fierce fighting had broken out in the province between Protestants and Catholics; the police in Belfast had shot many civilians; and in the Bogside area of Londonderry, besieged Catholics had put up barricades. When the troops arrived they were welcomed as protectors, and the barricades were taken down.

August 1969: the Bogside, a Catholic area of the mainly Protestant city of Londonderry, was virtually besieged by hostile neighbours and police. The 'Battle of the Bogside' was a key factor in the decision by the British government to send troops into Northern Ireland.

Origin of the conflict

Northern Ireland's problems were rooted in the 300-year period when Britain ruled all of Ireland and hostility between Catholics and Protestants created deeply divided communities. In 1921 most of Ireland became self-governing and eventually transformed itself into an independent, overwhelmingly Catholic republic.

The north, where Protestants were a majority, remained part of the UK. Though subject to the British government, it had its own parliament at Stormont and was mostly left to manage its own affairs. Stormont rule was nakedly unjust. The political system was manipulated to deny any influence to the large Catholic minority (about a third of the population), which was discriminated against in job and housing provision. The police (RUC) and a volunteer reserve (B Specials) were instruments of this Protestant, or 'Loyalist' regime. The only resistance came from the IRA (Irish Republican Army), a militant underground organization that had never accepted the partition of Ireland. However, its campaigns achieved little, and by the 1960s it was pursuing a political rather than a military strategy.

The Troubles

The situation was transformed in 1968 by the emergence of a civil rights movement, pledged to secure equal rights for all citizens in the province. But civil rights demonstrations and marches were brutally assaulted, with the RUC and the B Specials prominent among the attackers. The British government pressed the Northern Irish authorities to put through reforms, but resistance to any concessions was strong. Meanwhile, the situation began to deteriorate. A vicious attack on a New Year 1969 civil rights march led to mob violence on both sides, culminating in the disturbances that brought in British troops.

The 'temporary' army presence was prolonged as 'the Troubles' continued in earnest. The IRA resumed military activity, the army's good relations with the Catholic community collapsed, and the Ulster Volunteers and other Protestant equivalents to the IRA went into action. Decades of conflict ensued before the emergence of a peace process in the 1990s, which led to an end to the violence and the election of a joint Protestant–Catholic government in 2007.

British soldiers on a Northern Irish street. Welcomed at first, they soon became targets as the IRA and other armed groups stepped up their activities.

What the papers said

The decision to put British troops on to the riot-torn streets of Ulster is the right one. Vastly regrettable, but regrettably unavoidable. The government of Major James Chichester-Clark in Northern Ireland has had its chance to bring peace to the region. And it has failed. The first task for the troops is to help restore order. An unenviable job. As the men in the middle, their presence will be resented by extremists on both sides.

The Daily Mirror, 15 August 1969

FURTHER INFORMATION
Books:
Northern Ireland and England by Robert Cottrell (Chelsea House, 2005)
Websites:
www.bbc.co.uk/history/recent/troubles
An exploration of the Northern Ireland conflict

The First Day at Woodstock

Its official name was 'The Woodstock Music and Art Fair'. It was actually a festival of rock and folk music, the kind of event that regularly brought young people together in the 1960s. However, Woodstock was special, both in its size and in the mood it generated. Over 400,000 people – an extraordinary number – congregated on farmland near Bethel in New York State, USA. For three days, despite rain, mud and primitive facilities, they listened to famous performers such as Joan Baez; Janis Joplin; the Grateful Dead; Crosby, Stills and Nash; the Band; and, from Britain, the Who and Joe Cocker.

Woodstock was billed as 'three days of peace and music'. The emphasis on peace was not an accident, since mass opposition to the war in Vietnam was at its height and reinforced feelings among the young of being at odds with the older generation.

The huge crowd at Woodstock, almost all of them young people. Many believed that a new era of peace and love was beginning.

The hippy movement

In the early 1960s, the young had tended to enjoy the smart lifestyle and possessions made possible by Western affluence. As the decade went on, the mood changed. Some, especially students, became politically committed. But many others were attracted to hippy values, which encouraged the young to 'drop out' – to abandon conventional lives and careers in favour of a liberated lifestyle, often involving the use of perception-altering drugs and some form of communal living. Many more became 'weekend dropouts', dressing and living hippy-style during their leisure hours. Among this group there was a strong, idealistic belief that 'flower-power' and 'peace and love' could change the world without sustained struggle or violence.

A memorable event

Woodstock was one of the supreme expressions of this outlook, strongly felt by those who were there, and experienced through the film and album of the event by huge numbers who were not. The legendary climax of the event came on the unscheduled fourth morning, when guitarist Jimi Hendrix played a two-hour set in front of a remaining audience of 80,000. At moments in his inventive rendering of the US national anthem, *The Star-Spangled Banner*, he produced sounds like explosions and machine-gun fire, clearly intended to evoke US actions in Vietnam. Woodstock is still remembered for the quality of the music performed and the mood it captured, soon to change as more violent confrontations occurred and different values started to take hold.

Jimi Hendrix playing his legendary two-hour set on 18 August, the morning after the official end of the Woodstock festival.

What the papers said

The dreams of marijuana and rock music that drew 300,000 fans and hippies … had little more sanity than the impulses that drive the lemmings to march to their deaths in the sea. They ended in a nightmare of mud and stagnation that paralysed Sullivan County for a whole weekend. Surely parents, the teachers and indeed all the adults who helped to create the society which these young people are so feverishly rebelling [against] must bear some responsibility for this outrageous episode.

The New York Times, 16 August 1969

- **SEE ALSO**
  Pages 18–19: 8 February 1964:
  Beatlemania Hits the USA
  Pages 20–21: 8 March 1965:
  The Marines Arrive in Vietnam
  Pages 30–31: 10 May 1968:
  Barricades Rise in Paris

- **FURTHER INFORMATION**
  Books:
  Woodstock
  by Louise Gerdes (Greenhaven Press, 2011)
  Websites:
  www.woodstock.com/themusic.php
  The Woodstock Festival

30 JULY 1966

England's World Cup Victory

In 1966, England was the host country for football's greatest prize, the World Cup. Sixteen teams competed for the trophy, including the strongly fancied Argentine, Portuguese and West German sides. England had never won the cup, but the team seemed to have a good chance with outstanding players such as skipper Bobby Moore, Bobby Charlton and goalkeeper Gordon Banks. England won its group and then had to work hard to defeat Argentina in the quarter finals and Portugal in the semi-finals. England's opponents in the final were West Germany, who had disposed of Uruguay and the Soviet Union. The final took place at Wembley Stadium on 30 July before a crowd of almost 97,000.

There were two early goals, by West Germany's Helmut Haller and England's Geoff Hurst. Most of the game was then dominated by tight defensive play. With 12 minutes to go, a shot from Hurst rebounded off German fullback Weber, and Martin Peters slammed it into the net. England continued to attack, but in the final minute Weber had his revenge with a deftly taken equalizer.

England player Roger Hunt raises his arms in jubilation after a shot from Geoff Hurst hit the crossbar of the West German goal and bounced down. Hunt believed the ball had crossed the goal line, and the referee agreed. England went on to win the match, and the World Cup.

Did it cross the line?

In extra time, both teams were visibly fighting against exhaustion. Alan Ball chased a long pass from Nobby Stiles, trapped the ball close to the corner and crossed it to Hurst. Trying to control it, Hurst leaned back so far that he actually toppled over. His shot hit the underside of the goal bar, fell onto the goal line and then spun away into the field. Had it crossed the line before that? The referee and linesman conferred, then the referee decided that Hurst had scored. The Germans protested hotly at the time and the decision was fiercely debated for years afterwards.

As the end of extra time approached, the Germans staked everything on desperate attacks; England needed only to play out time. In the closing seconds, Moore cleared the ball with a long kick, Hurst booted it hard – and it went into the net. Hurst became the first player to score a hat-trick in a World Cup final, and England ran out winners by 4-2.

A legendary event

The 1966 final was a dramatic encounter, and England rejoiced at the national team's first-ever tournament victory. Over the next 40 years, despite some moments of high hope, England failed to win the cup again, and as a result their 1966 triumph became a legendary event.

Captain Bobby Moore flourishes the World Cup as he is carried on the shoulders of his teammates. Also pictured are (left to right) Nobby Stiles, Jack Charlton, Alan Ball, Martin Peters, Geoff Hurst, Ray Wilson, George Cohen and Bobby Charlton.

eye witness

The match was practically over. Kenneth Wolstenholme was telling a nation glued to their TV sets, 'Some people are on the pitch … they think it's all over.'… It was at this point that I decided to hit the ball with every last ounce of strength I had … just as I shaped to kick the ball it hit a divot, bouncing up fractionally higher than I was anticipating. This meant that I caught it on the hard part of my instep and it flew into the net. Wolstenholme continued his famous piece of commentary: 'It is now!'

Sir Geoff Hurst describes the final moments of the match in *1966 and All That*, written with Michael Hart (Headline Book Publishing, 2006 [revised edition])

• **FURTHER INFORMATION**
  Books:
  England '66: The 1966 World Cup in Photographs
  by Ray Tedman
  (Reynolds & Hearn, 2010)
  Websites:
  www.fifa.com/worldcup/archive/edition=26/index.html
  FIFA World Cup 1966

The Aberfan Disaster

At about 9.15 am, there was a noise like a thunderclap above the village of Aberfan in South Wales. It was so loud that it could be heard 150 kilometres away. Almost at once, vast amounts of slimy black sludge began pouring into the village. The sludge came from a slag heap, 180 metres high, that stood beside Aberfan.

In the 1960s, coal mining was still a major British industry, and it had long been the main source of employment in the valleys of South Wales, where mining villages grew up close to the pits. When coal was excavated and brought to the surface, quantities of waste came up with it. The waste was separated from the coal and dumped nearby. In time, hundreds of these tips accumulated, creating strange, artificial mountain landscapes throughout the mining districts.

Aberfan's shattered village school can be seen behind the helpers working on the tip above it. They are filling and stacking sandbags to divert running water capable of starting another landslide.

Tip 7 collapses

The collapse of Aberfan's Tip 7 caused the disaster. Saturated with water, the waste became a semi-liquid black mass that flooded into the village. It swept away hillside trees and farm cottages, then poured across a disused canal and a railway embankment. Still unchecked, it hit the back of Pantglas junior school and engulfed it, broke through the school wall and destroyed 18 terraced houses before finally coming to a halt.

Terrible toll

The alarm spread quickly, and miners, police, firemen and ambulance services worked desperately hard through the day and night. Removing the sludge was difficult and dangerous, mostly resulting in the uncovering of dead bodies. The worst aspect of the situation was that the village children were already at school when the tip collapsed. There were some incredible escapes, but the final tally was heart-rending. Twenty-eight adults and 116 children were dead. Almost every family lost a relative, and the life of the village was scarred for decades.

Warnings ignored

After the disaster, an official enquiry revealed that many warnings about the stability of the tip had been ignored and that inspection arrangements were inadequate. The waste had been dumped close to the mining villages to save money, and safety measures had been neglected for the same reason. The authority responsible for the industry, the National Coal Board, found that another hundred tips were dangerous and, late in the day, set about making them safe. Although the coal industry declined from the 1980s, large numbers of coal tips remain in mining areas, often remodelled and landscaped.

The grim face of a rescue worker, one of the many people who tried to help when a tip collapsed and part of Aberfan village was engulfed. In a small community, such a disaster hit every family hard.

eye witness

The mountain had reached the school by the time I got downstairs and I dashed the 20 yards to the playground. Just as I got in the school I saw two little girls. They were terror stricken. As I grabbed them and turned to take them outside I could see other children cowering under desks. By the time I got the two girls ... away from the school and gone back it was too late to help anyone else. The mountain had moved over the school.

Bernard Chamberlain, a miner, quoted in the *Daily Mail*, 22 October 1966

• **FURTHER INFORMATION**

📖 Books:
Aberfan: The Days After: A Journey in Pictures by I C Rapoport (Parthian Books, 2005)

Websites:
www.nuffield.ox.ac.uk/politics/aberfan/home.htm
The Aberfan disaster archive site

Chichester Completes an Epic Voyage

Francis Chichester on the deck of his yacht Gipsy Moth IV, *making preparations for his epic solo voyage. The route would take him from Plymouth to Sydney and then, via Cape Horn, back to Plymouth.*

Sir Francis Chichester ended his 43,000-kilometre voyage in style. Beacons along the English coast guided his yacht into Plymouth harbour, where a quarter of a million people waited to cheer him on during the final moments. His triumphant arrival on 28 May 1967 was the culmination of a nine-month epic of skill and endurance.

Chichester was not a conventional hero. At the start of his voyage he was a spare, bespectacled figure, almost 66 years old. But he was a seasoned adventurer with a colourful past as a pioneer aviator, wartime flyer and transatlantic yacht racer. As a pilot he had flown Gipsy Moth aircraft, and he used the name for all of his yachts.

A solo circumnavigation

The latest *Gipsy Moth* was specially built for Chichester when he decided on a supreme adventure – a solo voyage round the world. On 27 August 1966, Chichester sailed out of the Cornish port of Plymouth and into the Atlantic. *Gipsy Moth IV* was a high-tech vessel with useful safety features and self-steering gear that enabled the solo voyager to rest and sleep. But the trip was hazardous all the same, and even before leaving the Bay of Biscay Chichester had sustained a serious leg injury.

The trade winds carried *Gipsy Moth IV* effortlessly south and past the Cape of Good Hope. As the vessel swung east, it was driven along by the ferocious 'Roaring Forties', winds that often reached gale force. The constant battle against the elements put a terrible strain on Chichester, increased when the self-steering broke and could only be partially fixed. Chichester pressed on across the Indian Ocean and through the Bass Strait that separates Australia and Tasmania. He made landfall in Sydney on 12 December, 107 days after leaving Plymouth.

The greatest test

Chichester's already remarkable achievement was recognized by the award of a knighthood. But there was more to come. *Gipsy Moth IV* left Sydney on 29 January 1967, heading into the vastness of the Pacific. The vessel survived severe storms, but the greatest test of all was rounding the notoriously stormy Cape Horn. Chichester made this part of the voyage without sleep, steering and remaining vigilant all the way. Once into the Atlantic there were few difficulties, although towards the end *Gipsy Moth IV* was becalmed and progress was maddeningly slow. But Chichester's reception as he sailed into Plymouth harbour must have made up for everything he had endured. He had made a solo voyage round the world faster, and with fewer stops, than any seafarer before him. His record has since been broken.

Home again and now knighted: Sir Francis Chichester waves to a large crowd from the balcony of the Mansion House, London. He holds up a medallion showing his yacht Gipsy Moth IV, *presented to him by the Lord Mayor.*

 eye witness

I woke up as we began to roll and said to myself 'Well, here she goes'. It was pitch black ... everything started falling from what was normally down to what was normally up. I was on the downside and the whole boat was above me. Bottles, tins and bags of fruit shot out to where the bunk had been.... Knives and crockery showered on to me across the cabin.... I was very, very lucky.... I escaped with only a cut lip. There was never any question *Gipsy Moth* would right herself.... The question was, which way would she come up?

Sir Francis Chichester's account of the worst moment, in *Life* magazine, 9 June 1967

- **FURTHER INFORMATION**
- 📖 Books:
  Gipsy Moth IV: A legend sails again by Paul Gelder (Wiley Nautical, 2007)
- 🖰 Websites:
  http://news.bbc.co.uk/onthisday/hi/dates/stories/may/28/newsid_2495000/2495799.stm
  Chichester completes his voyage

People of the Decade

Moshe Dayan
(1915–1981)
Born in British-ruled Palestine, Dayan joined the underground Jewish army. He fought in World War II, adopting his distinctive black patch after losing an eye. After Israel's establishment in 1948, he quickly rose through the ranks. As chief of staff he planned the 1956 Israeli campaign against Egypt. In 1967 he was appointed minister of defence and became chief architect of Israel's victory in the Six-Day War. Later in his political career, however, he advocated giving back most of the conquered territories.

Betty Friedan
(1921–2006)
American writer Betty Friedan was convinced that many women were (like herself) dissatisfied with their lives. In *The Feminine Mystique* (1963) she argued that society forced them into dependency on men and limited roles as wives, mothers and home-makers. Highly controversial at the time, the book is now recognized as a pioneering feminist text. Friedan was also an active campaigner, co-founding and leading influential bodies such as the National Organization for Women (NOW).

Ernesto 'Che' Guevara
(1928–1963)
Angered by mass poverty, Argentine-born Guevara supported radical causes in Guatemala and then in Cuba, where he fought alongside Fidel Castro against the Fulgencio Batista dictatorship. After Castro's 1959 victory, Guevara held government posts until his departure from Cuba in 1965. He hoped to start new revolutions, first in the Congo and then in Bolivia. In Bolivia, however, he was wounded, captured and shot. Posters made his image world-famous and turned him into a legend.

Lyndon Baines Johnson
(1908–1973)
A Texan, Johnson became a senator and a leading member of the Democratic Party. From 1961 he was John F Kennedy's vice-president, taking over as president when Kennedy was assassinated in November 1963. As the champion of the 1964 Civil Rights Act and other reforms, Johnson visualized the USA as 'the Great Society'. He won the 1964 presidential election, but his second term was mired in controversy over his commitment to the Vietnam War.

John F Kennedy
(1917–1963)
In 1960, American politician John F Kennedy became the nation's first Roman Catholic president. At a time when politicians were mostly elderly, he was relatively young, as well as wealthy and good looking; he and his wife Jackie were seen as uniquely glamorous. Kennedy pursued liberal policies and ably handled the 1962 Cuban Missile Crisis. His assassination shocked the world. His brother Robert (1925–1968) was also assassinated in the middle of his political career.

Martin Luther King, Jr
(1929–1968)
Baptist minister Martin Luther King, Jr was the leader of the civil rights movement to secure equality for black Americans. Originally based in Montgomery, Alabama, he led demonstrations, boycotts and marches in the American South, using non-violent resistance to unjust laws. The 1964 Civil Rights Act and 1965 Voting Rights Act were largely the result of his efforts. In 1964 King was awarded the Nobel Peace Prize, but four years later he was shot by an assassin.

Nikita Sergeyevich Khrushchev
(1894–1971)
Soviet politician Nikita Khrushchev effectively became sole leader of his country from 1955. He ended the reign of terror associated with the dictatorship of Joseph Stalin (died 1953), but opposition to Communist Party rule continued to be forbidden. Though pugnacious and erratic, Khrushchev pulled back from the brink of war during the 1962 Cuban Missile Crisis and improved relations with the USA. He lost power in 1964 and was forced to retire.

Mao Zedong
(1893–1976)
One of the founders of the Chinese Communist Party (1921), Mao became its unchallenged leader when the communist forces were threatened with annihilation, and he led them on a famous 9,650-kilometre 'Long March' to safety (1934–1936). After the communist victory in 1949, Mao became head of the new Chinese People's Republic. He carried through major changes such as China's break with the Soviet Union and the Cultural Revolution, remaining in power until his death.

Glossary

apartheid The political system that operated in South Africa between 1948 and 1994. It separated the different peoples living there and gave special privileges to those of European origin.

atria Chambers in the heart that pump blood into the ventricles (*see* ventricles).

bloc A group of states, usually with similar political or economic values, that stand together.

blockade An organized action to seal off a state or territory, preventing people or goods from entering or leaving it.

B Specials The Ulster Special Constabulary – the reserve police force of Northern Ireland, abolished in 1970.

Cold War The state of nonviolent conflict between the Soviet Union and the United States and their respective allies between 1945 and 1990.

colony A territory ruled by another state. Until the 1960s, many parts of Africa were colonies of European states.

communism A system in which the state controls wealth and property. In practice, the Soviet Union and other communist states were run exclusively by their Communist Parties.

coup A sudden seizure of power.

decolonization The process by which states gave up their colonies, some more willingly than others.

democracy A system of government in which the leaders have been elected freely and equally by all the citizens of a country.

diabetes A group of diseases most commonly caused by excessive blood sugar.

dictatorship A political system in which a country is ruled by one person or a small group, without the consent of the people.

dogfights Combats between fighter aircraft.

elite A group or class that is especially gifted or privileged.

factions Groups inside a party or government that have opposing ideas or ambitions.

ghetto A term that originally described the area in many European cities where Jews were forced to live. It is now often used of slum areas in cities anywhere that are crowded with poor and disadvantaged groups.

guerrillas Fighters who wage hit-and-run warfare, usually against a stronger enemy. They often take advantage of a mountainous or jungle environment in which they can hide.

hippy A person who rejects conventional values and goals and believes in unversal peace and love.

IRA Irish Republican Army; until recently the IRA was an armed group that aimed to overthrow the Northern Irish state and unite the region with the Irish Republic.

KGB The secret police of the former Soviet Union.

Mafia A powerful criminal organization that originated in Italy and is very active in the USA.

militancy Actively, possibly aggressively, working for the triumph of ideas or beliefs.

napalm A chemical, including petroleum, which is highly inflammable. Napalm was much used, in flame throwers and bombs, by US forces in Vietnam.

NLF National Liberation Front for South Vietnam; the resistance force that fought against the government of President Ngo Dinh Diem in South Vietnam.

proletarian A communist term for a worker.

radical A person or policy favouring fundamental and far-reaching change.

RUC Royal Ulster Constabulary – the Northern Ireland police force (1922–2001).

segregation A situation in which different ethnic groups must use different public facilities (for example schools, transportation, park benches, toilets and cafés).

socialism A political system in which the main industries of a country are owned and run by the state for the general benefit.

Soviet Union Also known as the USSR (Union of Soviet Socialist Republics), a country consisting of Russia and a number of other East European, Baltic and Central Asian countries. The leading communist power, the Soviet Union existed from 1922 to 1991.

Stormont The parliament of Northern Ireland.

strafing Machine-gunning from a plane of installations or people on the ground.

ventricles Chambers in the heart that receive blood from the atria (*see* **atria**).

Index

Page numbers in **bold** refer to illustrations